MW00775026

THE DEPTHS OF
HUMILITY

A UNIQUE AND COMPREHENSIVE STUDY

"...as ye have come to the knowledge of the
glory of God... humble yourselves even in
the depths of humility..."

King Benjamin, Book of Mormon, Mosiah 4: 11

Larry A. Tyler

The Depths of Humility

Published by Dox Marketing, Meridian, Idaho.

Printed in the U.S.A.
First Edition

Cover artwork: Brodie Tyler
Cover photo: © bastan / Fotolia
larrytyler2@9mail.com

CONTENTS

INTRODUCTION

One night, while contemplating the topic of humility, I had the following vision. I was standing in the doorway of a nearly empty room, when a gap in the floor opened up in front of me, about three feet wide, allowing me to see into the room below. I had not previously known that there was a lower floor in the building. I knew then that the lower room represented a deeper level of humility than where I was standing. I knew that many people were on my same floor, but was immediately impacted that the deeper level of humility could be and should be achieved. Although the concept of different levels of humility is simple and logical and certainly not new, the visual impact of that experience has been and will continue to be powerful in my life. As an old man I regret that it has taken me so many years to learn this lesson.

As I continued my study of humility I was surprised to find how few lessons, talks, articles or even books there are on the subject . Even with computer searches, surprisingly little is to be found, giving the importance of the topic. Humility is often mentioned, and scriptures are often quoted along with the teaching of other topics, but any in-depth complete study of the subject still evades my search. What is humility? How deep is deep? What keeps us from being humble? How is humility acquired? Even lessons on pride, the opposite of humility, and important to our understanding, are few and far between. It's almost as though Ezra Taft Benson had said everything there was to say or understand about pride in his landmark address, "Beware of Pride", in 1989, so only the mention of the word is needed. It is as though everybody is presumed to already know everything there is to know about humility, so just the mention of the word or quoting an occasional scripture is sufficient.

Not being a scholar or an intellectual, my approach is more practical. I believe that the answers to our problems of pride, complacency, greed, selfishness and even divorce have already been given to us. What we need are more ears to hear *(Matthew 13:9)*. Since that which we need to know, about in-depth humility, has not been capsulated for our consumption and benefit, we must glean a little here and a little there from our Lord's teachings, prophets and the scriptures. Hence, this book quotes many scriptures, along with quotes from General Authorities. To our advantage, doctrines and the pattern of humility are constant and unchanging. But men sometimes overcomplicate simple issues, cures and causes, thus creating a need to return to the basics. In-depth-humility, I believe to be one of those basics. To understand humility we must also understand pride.

It should be well noted that not everyone sees humility as a strength. In much of the everyday world of business and academia, it is thought to be a weakness. Since our society tends to greatly value the learning of men and even requires higher degrees from institutions of higher learning as a threshold for qualification to teach, write and council, a reluctance to teach all the relative factors surrounding humility is apparently innate and inevitable. I am a simple man, the last one my friends would ever expect to write a book. But I feel called to write on those subjects which cannot be found otherwise. I could not write this myself alone, as small as it is, and hesitate to call it "my book".

Some believe that a book must be embellished so as not to be a "pamphlet". But...

...the Lord sent forth the fullness of his gospel, his everlasting covenant, reasoning in plainness and simplicity.
» *D&C 133:57*

I would prefer that we keep it that way. No attempt has been made to expand or embellish. I call this a "book" because it is large in concept. Hopefully, because of its simplicity, and not having to plow through hundreds of pages, each reader will learn and retain more of the truths taught herein.

Great hidden danger lies as the philosophies of men are embraced, while the Depths of Humility are given less attention. And so it is against this headwind of our times that this little book teaches many factors surrounding humility, in-depth. Since pride is the opposite of humility, this subject is also addressed throughout the book.

Putting-off pride and becoming truly humble is not something which we accomplish once and feel good about and forget. It is to be a life-long pursuit, keeping and adding to our humility as we serve and learn precept upon precept. May each reader learn more of the patterns to avoid and more of our Lord's patterns to follow, to help them. May each reader truly put-off pride and be encompassed into the "The Depths of Humility".

Larry A. Tyler

CHAPTER 1
THE DEPTHS OF HUMILITY

The title of this work is taken from the words of King Benjamin:

> *And again I say unto you as I have said before, that as ye have come to the knowledge of the glory of God... humble yourselves even in the depths of humility...*
> » *Mosiah 4:11.*

This scripture implies that there are different levels of humility, with the direct admonition to seek for the greater depth. With great depths in the offering, it behooves us to learn all that we can about this personal virtue. Teachings of humility are nearly wasted on the wicked, but are greatly needed by the righteous.

It may be interesting that definitions of the word "humble" are not that easy to find. In Mormon Doctrine, Bruce R. McConkie gives no definition but relates it to meekness and patience. Our Bible dictionary has no listing for humility. From our church website, humility recognizes the need for dependence on our Lord.

One dictionary however, has a definition which probably more resembles our Lord's: "having a feeling of insignificance, inferiority, subservience, low in rank, importance, quality". Synonyms given are "lowliness, meekness, submissiveness".

It is sometimes easier to identify what humility is not as we see it in other people: arrogance, egotism, pretentiousness, self-importance, pride.

We are blessed with an abundance of scriptures concerning humility. Many are reprinted here, at least in part. Humility is necessary for supreme blessings in the hereafter. Becoming humble is more than just advisable, it is a commandment.

And again, by way of commandment to the church concerning the manner of baptism—All those who humble themselves before God, and desire to be baptized, and come forth with broken hearts and contrite spirits... shall be received by baptism into his church.

» *D&C 20:37*

From Spencer W. Kimball we learn:

"For the righteous, to be humble is not an option, it is required"

» *Teachings of Spencer W, Kimball Ch. 9*

...he that shall humble himself shall be exalted.

» *Matthew 23:12*

Humble yourselves therefore under the mighty hand of God, that he may exalt you in due time.

» *1 Peter 5:6*

...becometh as a child, submissive, meek, humble, patient... even as a child doth submit to his father.

» *Mosiah 3:19*

If my people, which are called by my name, shall humble themselves, and pray, and seek my face, and turn from their wicked ways; then will I hear from heaven and will forgive their sin, and will heal their land.

» *2 Chronicles 7:14*

Remember faith, virtue, knowledge, temperance, patience, brotherly kindness, godliness, charity, humility, diligence.

» *D&C 4:6*

Humility not only benefits us in our next estate but also helps us while in this realm.

Be thou humble; and the Lord thy God shall lead the by the hand, and give the answers to thy prayers.

» D&C 112:10

And if your brethren desire to escape their enemies, let them repent of all their sins, and become truly humble before me and contrite.

» D&C 54:3

When the early Saints were having problems paying their debts, the Lord gave them this promise.

And it is my will that you shall humble yourselves before me, and obtain this blessing by your diligence and humility and the prayer of faith.

» D&C 104:79

In the fifty and first year of the reign of the judges over the people of Nephi, prosperity had brought pride into the hearts of some of the people who professed to belong to the church. But there was a more humble part of the people. *(See Heleman 3:3-34)*

Nevertheless they did fast and pray oft, and did wax stronger and stronger in their humility, and firmer and firmer in the faith of Christ, unto the filling their souls with joy and consolation, yea, *even to the purifying and the <u>sanctification</u> of their hearts, which <u>sanctification</u> cometh because of their yielding their hearts unto God.*

» *Heleman 3:35 (Emphasis added)*

Becoming stronger in our humility and yielding our hearts unto God should lead us to sanctification.

"To be sanctified is to become clean, pure, and spotless; to be free from the blood and sins of the world; to become a new creature of the Holy Ghost, one whose body has been renewed by the rebirth of the Spirit."

» *Bruce R. McConkie, Mormon Doctrine, first edition, p. 608*

CHAPTER 2
HIS PATTERN OF HUMILITY

*And again, I will give unto you a pattern in all
things, that ye may not be deceived; for Satan is
abroad in the land, and he goeth forth deceiving
the nations.*

» *D&C 52:14*

Our Savior has given us a pattern to help us navigate
through the many subtle and often alluring deceptions
put in place by him who's duty it is to do so. This promise
comes with a warning. The promise is that He will give
us teachings which form a guide, a recognizable pattern,
to follow. The warning is that if we do not follow this
pattern, and use it to compare all things, we may be deceived, like much of the world today.

The pattern is given to the righteous and the wicked

alike, for all may be deceived. Great danger lies in feeling that one is above deception. From this scripture we should be mindful that Satan is real and the possibility of our deception is real. Our scriptures give us the admonition to "be not deceived", emphasizing the need to compare all things to His pattern. Nobody, regardless of success or position is immune to deception.

...by the sleight of men, and cunning craftiness, whereby they lie in wait to deceive.

» *Ephesians 4:14*

...Take heed that no man deceive you.

» *Matthew 24:4*

...Be not deceived...

» *1 Corinthians 6:9*

We have a great example of humility.

...Therefore, what manner of men ought ye to be? Verily I say unto you, even as I am.

» *3 Nephi 27:27 (Emphasis added)*

Was not our Savior a perfect example? We can ask ourselves, are we acting anything like our Savior would act in any given situation?

For I have given you an example, that ye should do as I have done to you.

» *John 13:15*

...I am meek and lowly in heart...
» *Matthew 11:29*

If He is meek and lowly in heart, both being forms of humility, should we not be also? Humility must become part of who we are after we have overcome other obstacles. But even for the devoutly religious, this characteristic is illusive and does not come easily or without test. Just being a Christian or a member of His true Church does not guarantee humility. It is possible to think we are humble when in actuality we are filled with pride. Prideful people can and do function quite well in a religiously structured environment; you probably know a few.

To carefully follow "His pattern" and avoid *all the cunning and the snares and the wiles of the devil (Heleman 3:29),* we must be alert, ever vigilant, watching on every front for look-alikes, imitations, false doctrines and even false educational ideas. We must not underestimate the ability of the great deceiver or drop our guard, even for a moment. Something of such great value as humility does not come easily. The better we know and understand our Lord's pattern the better we are able to compare all things. The better we are able to identify the dangerous deceptions in our path, the better we are able to protect ourselves. With desire and guidance from the Holy Spirit it is possible to discern the subtle deceptions, as black from white.

When was the last time you discovered a popular philosophy which does not match our Savior's pattern?

When was the last time you recognized a false doctrine or false educational idea?

Part of our Lord's pattern is for us to learn who and what we really are. *Remember the worth of souls is great in the sight of God (D&C 18:10).* Just because we are of great worth in the sight of God does not mean that we should view ourselves that way; teachings in our Lord's pattern are very much different. As soon as we begin to enjoy the feeling of great worth, in comes the pride and out goes the humility. It is a paradox.

"In and of ourselves we are but a lifeless lump of clay."

» *Joseph F. Smith, Conference, October 1899*

O how great is the nothingness of the children of men; yea, even they are less than the dust of the earth.

» *Helaman 12:7*

King Benjamin taught his people:

And again I say unto you as I have said before, that as ye have come to the knowledge of the glory of God, or if ye have known of his goodness and have tasted of his love, and have received a remission of your sins, which causeth such exceedingly great joy in your souls, even so I would that ye should remember, and always retain in remembrance, the greatness of God, and <u>your own nothingness,</u>

and his goodness and long-suffering towards you, unworthy creatures, and humble yourselves even in the <u>depths of humility</u>, calling on the name of the Lord daily, and standing steadfastly in the faith of that which is to come, which was spoken by the mouth of the angel.

» *Mosiah 4:11 (Emphasis added)*

Ammon said:

Yea, I know that I am nothing; as to my strength I am weak; therefore I will not boast of myself, but I will boast of my God, for in his strength I do all things...

» *Alma 26:12*

Having heard or read these scriptures many times before, which of us can say that we did not just nod our head in agreement, all the while feeling that they do not apply to us today, in our time? After all, this is a day when the philosophies of men teach us that we should raise our own self-perception, not lower it. Self-pride is worshipped in the halls of academia to be of great value and cure-all for most social problems. Certainly, many have traded their depression for a portion of pride. Suggesting that we should consider ourselves as less, not more, unfortunately brings criticism for putting ourselves down. "For we are children of God, and therefore of great worth", goes the refrain.

Reconciling these two philosophies is a challenge worthy of any man. On the one hand, we have experienced a lifetime of indoctrination that mother and dad are so proud of us, that we are to win over our competitors, rewarded, revered and envied for our superiority. On the other, we have the simple teachings and pattern of Jesus Christ, often given lip service but not always embraced, that we are of ourselves less than the dust of the earth *(Heleman 12:7)*. Such is the test of acquiring humility in our day and the difficulty of throwing-off all pride. It is not too late to trade some pride for a little in-depth humility.

When man truly recognizes his own personal nothingness, he comes face to face with the fact that he must rely on the Lord. This is effective humility in action. This is faith in action.

Spencer W. Kimball taught, "I am the hole in the doughnut" *(Teachings of Spencer W. Kimball p. 233)*.

Trust in the Lord with all thine heart; and lean not unto thine own understanding.
    » *Proverbs 3:5*

May each reader guard himself against deception by comparing all things to "His pattern". May each reader come to grips with the paradox of man, that he is nothing, though valued greatly by our Maker. May we each avoid the trap of relying too much on the arm of flesh, the intellect and philosophies of men. May our understanding of our nothingness cause us to rely more each day on our Heavenly Father and His Son, Jesus Christ.

CHAPTER 3
A FAMILY OF VIRTUES

The word Humility stands at the head of a family of related virtues. Like those in any family, there are similarities, while each member is a little different with particular characteristics of their own. As we become more familiar with each virtue, we better understand what is expected of us. Knowing all the virtues makes the pattern of our Lord clear and prepares us to defend against deception and return to our Heavenly Home.

Charity

"Above all the attributes of godliness and perfection, charity is the one most devoutly to be desired."

> » Bruce R. McConkie, Mormon Doctrine, first edition, p. 114

Charity is also a widely misunderstood virtue. It is not just being generous and sharing our means with others. True charity is shown when we are kind to each other, considerate of each other's feelings and willing to help. It is best acquired by forgetting self, and being aware of others, their thoughts, needs and desires. Charity can show in our countenance and actions each day.

And to godliness brotherly kindness; and to brotherly kindness charity.

» *2 Peter 1:7*

Meekness

The virtue of meekness is often misunderstood.

"Few virtues have such inherent worth as meekness, for the meek are the god-fearing and the righteous. They are the ones who willingly conform to the gospel standards, thus submitting their wills to the will of the Lord. They are not the fearful, the spiritless, the timid. Rather, the most forceful, dynamic personality who ever lived—He who drove out the money changers from the temple, and with violence threw down their merchandising equipment (Matt. 21:12-13)--said of Himself. 'I am meek and lowly in heart.' (Matt. 11:29)."

» *Bruce R. McConkie, Mormon Doctrine, first edition, p. 430*

Blessed are the meek: for they shall inherit the earth.

> » *Mattew 5:5 (see also Psalms 37:11 and 3 Nephi 12:5)*

Put on therefore... meekness, longsuffering;

> » *Colossians 3:12*

Patience and long-suffering

Our degree of patience may reveal something of our level of humility. Many struggle with this virtue not understanding the connection to the family of virtues or the depths of humility.

Be patient in afflictions, revile not against those that revile.

> » *D&C 31: 9*

The natural man has the inclination to strike back at those who criticize, inconvenience or make fun of him, whether just or unjust. Revenge may even be considered. But we are advised to bear it up well, whether it be a major incident or simple occurrence, as with family, friends or strangers. We are to use Christ as our example.

...I would exhort you to have patience, and that ye bear with all manner of afflictions...

> » *Alma 34:40*

Full of love

There is much we can learn about love, but for this writing suffice it to say that we must have love for all of God's children.

...be led by the Holy Spirit, becoming humble, meek, submissive, patient, full of love and all long-suffering...
» *Alma 13:28*

And no one can assist in this work except he shall be humble and full of love...
» *D&C 12:8*

Broken Heart and Contrite Spirit

A broken heart is to feel extreme sorrow. Feeling contrite has to do with feeling sincere remorse for whatever sins we may have committed. It is to feel repentant.

...And whoso cometh unto me with a broken heart and a contrite spirit, him will I baptize with fire and with the Holy Ghost...
» *3 Nephi 9:20*

We can renew this covenant each time we partake of the Sacrament.

Poor in Spirit

To be poor in spirit is to be humble and teachable. Though we may feel persecuted or downtrodden or un- loved, we will be blessed.

Yea, blessed are the poor in spirit who come unto me, for theirs is the kingdom of heaven.

» *3 Nephi 12:3, (see also Matthew 5:3)*

Slow to offence

It has been said that a truly humble man cannot be offended. Being corrected is an opportunity to learn.

Gratitude

Following the cleansing of the ten lepers, only one returned to thank the Lord. No doubt all were grateful, but only one expressed that gratitude. We are indebted to the Lord for all he has done for us, and need to express our gratitude.

And now, in the first place, he hath created you, and granted unto you your lives, for which ye are indebted unto him.

» *Mosiah 2:23*

And ye must give thanks unto God in the Spirit for whatsoever blessing ye are blessed with.

» *D&C 46:32*

Awareness of Others

The ability to disengage from our own interest or activities sufficient to look at what is going on around us, is a virtue. Being aware of others and their needs opens an opportunity to help, assist and serve. It may be as simple as a friendly word, or not blocking a corridor, or noticing a neighbor in need. To stop what we are doing out of consideration of others is a selfless thing to do. It is a virtue which can be developed, garnering love and joy for all.

What a great family! Each virtue matches His pattern of humility. These are the characteristics He requires of us, which we should make part of who we are, that we may enter into the depths of humility and be more like Him.

CHAPTER 4
THE FORGOTTEN PRINCIPLE

Of all the principles taught by Jesus Christ, one is most likely the least-studied, least taught and least understood. A principle is a rule of action, conduct or law, and we know that all laws come with specific predicated blessings *(D&C 130: 20)*. This little-understood and nearly forgotten principle has its special blessings which are much needed in these perilous times. But the philosophies of men run contrary to this principle, and thus, it is largely ignored and nearly forgotten and subsequently misunderstood. The "forgotten principle" is the doctrine that we all need to "abase ourselves", as taught in ancient and modern scripture. The relationship between abasing and humbling becomes clear when all related scriptures are studied.

*He that exalteth himself shall be abased, and he
that abaseth himself shall be exalted.*

» *D&C 101:42*

*And whosoever shall exalt himself shall be abased;
and he that shall humble himself shall be exalted.*

» *Matthew 23:12*

*For whosoever exalteth himself shall be abased;
and he that humbleth himself shall be exalted.*

» *Luke 14:11*

A reader may note that the ancient scripture uses the
word humbleth, while modern scripture uses the word
abaseth. Understanding self-abasement is really quite
easy. Definitions show that, just as pride is elevating ourselves above others, self-abasement is simply to esteem
others above ourselves. To those formally trained in
the social sciences, the idea of abasing oneself is absurd
and runs contrary to everything they have been taught
in academia. So also do teachings of one's nothingness
and being humble, meek, contrite and lowly in heart run
contrary to secular teachings. This is further evidence
that some of the philosophies of men dominate our society today explaining why we are repeatedly warned about
them. And this is where deception starts.

A scripture well worth repeating, Paul reminds us:
*...in lowliness of mind let each esteem other better than
themselves (Philippians 2:3).* Contrary to secular teach-

ings, it is best that we think of ourselves as less, not more, lower, not higher, following better our Lord's pattern.

Self-abasement is not a weakness, or putting yourself down or hiding in a corner, but a strength. It is the ability to fend off self-absorption and pride, maintain humility. Self-abasement and humility go together, indeed, are inseparable.

Christ taught this principle clearly, by word and by parable to different people, ancient and modern. Even with the abundance of scriptural teachings on self-abasement, most teachers avoid the topic completely. In actuality, this principle is one of the great precepts which mortal man can possess, because it requires great humility and opens the door to spiritual gifts and understanding. It places us exactly where we should be in our relationship with other men and our Heavenly Father. It causes us to rely on Him. Just as humility is a strength, self-abasement has great power; power to draw upon the Holy Ghost with all His abilities.

In the Parable of the Wedding Guests *(Luke 14:7-11)*, Jesus taught that when we are invited to a wedding, we should sit in the lower room and not to presume to sit in the higher room until we are bade to do so; not to put ourselves forward because there may be a more honorable man bade to do so. Concluding in verse 11: *For whosoever exalteth himself shall be abased; and he that humbleth himself shall be exalted.*

In speaking of this specific verse, Luke 14:11, Bruce R. McConkie said:

"In a sense, Jesus here summarizes the whole plan and purpose of this mortal probation. It is to test men and see whether they will seek for worldly things---wealth, learning honors, power—or whether they will flee from pride, humble themselves before God and walk before him with an eye single to His glory. Without this basic Christian virtue of humility there is neither spiritual progression here nor eternal life hereafter."

> » *Doctrinal New Testament Commentary, p. 500)*

Brigham Young taught,

"It seems to be absolutely necessary in the providence of him who created us, and who organized and fashioned all things according to his wisdom, that man must descend below all things. It is written of the Savior in the Bible that he descended below all things that he might ascend above all."

> » *Journal of Discourses Vol. 15:3*

Nephi abased himself:

...O wretched man that I am! Yea, my heart

sorroweth because of my flesh; my soul grieveth because of mine iniquities.

I am encompassed about, because of the temptations and the sins which do so easily beset me.

And when I desire to rejoice, m heart groaneth because of my sins; nevertheless, I know in whom I have trusted.
   » *2 Nephi 4:17-19*

Ammon abased himself:

Yea, I know that I am nothing; as to my strength I am weak...
   » *Alma 26:12*

Paul abased himself:

For I am the least of the apostles, that I am not meet to be called an apostle...
   » *1 Corinthians 15:9*

King Benjamin abased himself:

And I, even I, whom you call you king, am no better than ye yourselves are; for I am also of the dust...
   » *Mosiah 2:26*

Self-abasing is being able to admit that you are not

the best, the smartest, the most talented, the best looking, the richest and being comfortable with that knowledge. Self-abasing withdraws you from competition. You are at peace when others excel over you; there is no jealously. With abasement, you are relieved from having to pretend you are something you are not, because of concern for what other people may think. With abasement, you can know that any strength you have comes from God. Self-abasement can bring comfort and confidence knowing you are still on course. Public self-abasement, when done properly, helps the audience relate to the speaker; they enjoy the honesty and lack of pride.

Self-basement enables exaltation. Self-abasing enables one to make upward progress, gaining precept upon precept without becoming prideful. Abasement negates the need to strive for a higher self-perception, because something much better is already possessed. Refusing to compete with others enables one to be more concerned for their neighbor and be happy for them when they excel.

In 1837, the Lord told Thomas B. Marsh, president of the Quorum of the Twelve Apostles, that there were some things in his heart in which He was not well pleased; then told him:

> *Nevertheless, inasmuch as thou hast abased thyself thou shalt be exalted; therefore, all thy sins are forgiven thee.*
> » *D&C 112:3*

Abasing and exalting were understood and taught in Old Testament times:

Thus saith the Lord God; Remove the diadem, and take off the crown: this shall not be the same: exalt him that is low, and abase him that is high.

» *Ezekial 21:26*

And the Lord told his servant Amos Davies, in 1838:

And when he shall prove himself faithful in all things that shall be entrusted unto his care, yea, even a few things, he shall be made ruler over many;

Let him therefore abase himself that he may be exalted. Even so. Amen.

» *D&C 124:113-114*

King Benjamin taught the multitude abasement even after they had received a remission for their sins:

...I would that ye should remember, and always retain in remembrance, the greatness of God, and your own nothingness, and his goodness and long-suffering towards you, unworthy creatures, and humble yourselves even in the depths of humility, calling on the name of the Lord daily, and standing steadfastly in the faith of that which is to come, which was spoken by the mouth of the angel.

» *Mosiah 4:11*

"Abasement" is so little understood, even our computer spell-check thinks it is a below-ground dwelling. Definition differences between abasing and debasing are negligible. Although doing it to ourselves is recommended, doing it to another will bring condemnation.

Self-abasement is a powerful form of humility, waiting to be used by His servants, with great promise of eternal blessings. It matches our Lord's pattern that we be not deceived.

Discourse by Apostle George Q. Cannon:

"If you go to the Lord with a broken heart and a contrite spirit, he will show to you all your faults, and all your weaknesses, he will bring plainly before you wherein you have come short in doing his will, and when you see yourself in the light of that spirit instead of being filled with pride, you will feel to abase yourselves and bring yourselves down in the very dust of humility; your own unworthiness will be so plain before you, that if pride should come into your heart at any time, you will almost be shocked at it, and you will feel to put it away from you. It is in this way that we as Latter-day Saints should live."

» *Journal of Discourses vol. 22:103*

CHAPTER 5
A VOICE FROM THE DUST

For those who shall be destroyed shall speak unto them out of the ground, and their speech shall be low out of the dust, and their voice shall be as one that hath a familiar spirit; for the Lord God will give unto him power, that he may whisper concerning them, even as it were out of the ground; and their speech shall whisper out of the dust.

» *2 Nephi 26:16*

This poetic prophecy refers of course to the Book of Mormon, which has a familiar spirit and gives us power. Power not to be proud of, but power which comes from understanding, wisdom and knowledge. The Nephites never had the Book of Mormon to help them, because it was not written for them; it was written specifically for us in our day. We are to learn from their experiences.

It has been said that if you listen to an old man for just a few minutes he will summarize the wisdom he has accumulated during his entire lifetime. With the Book of Mormon we not only have the wisdom of many prophets and the experience of entire civilizations, but we have additional words of our Savior and a far better understanding of "His pattern". Although the Nephites dwindled in unbelief we still have their wisdom whispering to us from the dust, that which we need to know, today in our day.

Perhaps the one most powerful lesson we can draw from The Book of Mormon is that factor which caused them to dwindle in unbelief. When the Nephites were truly humble they were invincible, but when pride overtook them, the Lamanites were able to defeat them.

When we ignore the pattern our Lord has given us, our values can easily reverse, and pride can actually be looked to as desirable. Oh, the words and the names change, as the wisdom of man is worshiped and the philosophies of men are embraced, but it always comes out as pride, in subtle deceit.

If we learn nothing more from The Book of Mormon than the lesson of pride we will profit greatly. May the understanding of pride spark a desire to seek after and acquire the personal virtue of in-depth humility.

...beware of pride, lest ye become as the Nephites of old.

» *D&C 38:39*

CHAPTER 6

A CLOSER LOOK AT PRIDE

We have been taught to beware of it, to put it away, to avoid a proud look, that only by it cometh contention, that it goeth before destruction, that it can destroy our soul and much more. With so many serious warnings about pride, it surely deserves a close examination.

As parents, we become proud of our children and freely tell them so. But the last thing we want them to do is carry over our pride and become prideful themselves. This is a "paradox"! Although, the worth of souls is great in the sight of God, the last thing Our Heavenly Father wants is for us is to be proud of it. This is the paradox of man. Better that we be humble and retain the understanding of our nothingness, than revel in our own self-worth.

In a recent General Conference, President Dieter F.

Uchtdorf taught us about our nothingness and the paradox of man.

> "The great deceiver knows that one of his most effective tools in leading the children of God astray is to appeal to the extremes of the paradox of man. To some, he appeals to their prideful tendencies, puffing them up and encouraging them to believe in the fantasy of their own self-importance and invincibility. He tells them they have transcended the ordinary and that because of ability, birthright, or social status, they are set apart from the common measure of all that surrounds them. He leads them to conclude that they are therefore not subject to anyone else's rules and not to be bothered by anyone else's problems."
>
> » *Pres. Dieter F. Uchtdorf, General Conference, October 2011*

With this understanding, we are better prepared to fend off the pride that is so frequently recommended to us through the intellect and philosophies of man. With the understanding of our own nothingness, and being meek and humble, we are more inclined to lean on the arm of our Lord and His understanding. This is His desire.

We are taught to beware of false prophets. Since all kinds of false doctrines, including teachings of pride, come through the philosophies of men, false prophets must be among our philosophers. Perhaps we have just been looking for strange looking men in long robes, or teachers from apostate groups, when we should have been looking in the natural habitat of philosophers, where they teach their congregations, in institutions of higher learning. Could the abundant warnings about being deceived, leaning on the arm of flesh, false educational ideas, intellect and philosophies of men be important clues to the cause of our prideful problems? Have we already been deceived with philosophies which encourage pride in self? Could the philosophies of men be causing us to think ~~to think~~ too much of ourselves? Should we not compare all of men's philosophies to the pattern of our Lord and reject those which are designed to deceive? Since the war with Satan is still raging, perhaps it would be a good idea to identify, collect and publish each detrimental philosophies of men (DPOM), that we may better know how to protect ourselves.

James E. Talmage, President Ezra Taft Benson and President David O. McKay have all commented on or used the term "righteous pride". On the face of things it might appear that they do not agree whether there is, or is not such pride. But in careful study there seems to emerge a fuller understanding of pride itself, not just righteous pride.

President David O. Mckay said in a General Priesthood meeting:

"I leave my blessing with you, my dear fellow

workers. Our hearts are full of pride—righteous pride—for the brotherhood exemplified last night by those young boys of the Aaronic Priesthood, and tonight by the tens of thousands of men holding the Melchizedek Priesthood."

» *Conference Report, October 1958*

The direction at which pride is aimed seems to make all the difference. Directed inward toward ourselves, pride is the evil of which we are amply warned, which has caused the loss of so many blessings and destroyed entire cultures. But directed outward, toward those who excel, our children when they make good choices, our leaders when they are valiant, our neighbors when they do well, can be *"a song of praise and thanksgiving to that Holy Being whose mercy endureth forever"* (Bruce R. McConkie, *Doctrinal New Testament Commentary*).

When this kind of pride is felt, it reflects humility, love and our willingness to esteem others above ourselves.

And so we have a choice to make; look inward with pride or retain our humility and find goodness in others of which we can be proud. Choose the first and expect to appear arrogant, conceited, self-loving, self-serving, seeking praise and notoriety. Choose the latter and prepare to enter into the depths of humility. Righteous pride may not be in the scriptures, as pointed out by President Benson in his "Beware of Pride" address, but prophets have shown us which way to aim it.

CHAPTER 7
FEELING HUMBLE

Some use the excuse that "if you feel humble, you have already lost it; so why try". We can do better than this! We can learn the correct pattern of how we are supposed to feel.

"...we must feel humble before God. ...we see how utterly helpless is the man who relies upon his own strength, his own experience and learning..."

» *Elder Rudger Clawson, Conference Report, April 1901*

"Though we may at times be stirred to anger, and our wrath move us to say and do things which are not pleasing in the sight of God, yet instantly, on regaining our sober senses and recovering from our lapse in to the power of darkness, we feel humble, repentant, and to ask forgiveness for the wrong that we have done to ourselves, and perchance to others."

> » President Lorenzo Snow, Conference Report, April 1898

"I feel humble and incapable, of my own strength, to accomplish the work that lies before me; but I have faith..."

> » Elder John A. Widtsoe, General Conference, October 1927

"I feel humble, beyond any language with which God has endowed me to express it, in standing before you here this morning...I stand here today in all humility, acknowledging my own weakness, my own lack of wisdom and information, and my lack of the ability to occupy the exalted position in which you have voted to sustain me."

> » President Heber J. Grant, Conference Report, June 1919

Elder Dallin H. Oaks teaches us not to be proud of our humility:

"Those who engage in self-congratulation over a supposed strength have lost the protection of humility and are vulnerable to Satan's using that strength to produce their downfall."

> » Dallin H. Oaks "Our Strengths Can Become Our Downfall" Ensign, Oct 1994, p.11

We have the option of feeling humble or proud; the best choice is obvious and we need not feel guilty.

CHAPTER 8
BARRIERS AND STUMBLING BLOCKS

By being aware of the barriers and stumbling blocks which stand in the way of humility, we are better able to acquire and retain this virtue.

Pride

As discussed in various parts of this book, pride is the great stumbling block in acquiring humility. By definition it is the opposite of humility. We cannot possess pride and humility in-depth at the same time. By commandment, we should not possess it at all.

> *Therefore, cease from all your... pride...*
> » *D&C 88:121*

It is possible to fully function and be advanced in the ranks of religion while holding a goodly portion of pride. Just because we are active and serve well does not indicate that we have little if it. The more prideful individuals are not normally aware of their problem, but often think of themselves as being humble. Everybody has at least some pride, but we cannot possess a lot of both pride and humility at the same time. Nobody will ever inquire of our level of pride, or humility. Judgments of our worthiness will be made using other criteria.

> *Behold, are ye stripped of pride? I say unto you, if ye are not ye are not prepared to meet God. Behold ye must prepare quickly; for the kingdom of heaven is soon at hand, and such an one hath not eternal life.*
>
> » *Alma 5:28*

The Natural Man

> *For the natural man is an enemy to God, and has been from the fall of Adam, and will be, forever and ever, unless he yields to the enticing of the Holy Spirit, and putteth off the natural man and becometh a saint through the atonement of Christ the Lord, and becometh as a child, submissive, meek, humble, patient, full of love, willing to submit to all things which the Lord seeth fit to inflict upon him, even as a child doth submit to his father.*
>
> » *Mosiah 3:19*

To be truly humble, we must each overcome the "natural man" in us. Learning our Lord's pattern of humility gives us something to fill the void left by our departing pridefulness.

Our Own Complacency

These have been good times, with relative peace at home and without serious persecution. We live in one of the few places on Earth where each couple, children or not, feel entitled to their own private home, multiple cars, relatively fine apparel, large screen H.D.T.V with/DVR, and leisure time, of course. Even our poor would appear wealthy when compared to most of this world's civilizations. And we have no real persecution to keep us on our toes. Such is the perfect incubator for complacency.

> *Complacency is "a feeling of quiet pleasure or security, often while unaware of some potential danger, or the like; self-satisfaction or smug satisfaction with an existing situation, condition, et."*
>
> *» Dictionary.com*

Our complacency was anticipated. The warning not to be "at ease" in Zion comes loud and clear from Nephi, as he saw what would come in our time. Complacency saps our motivation to continue to learn precept upon precept, for we tend to feel we have enough. It takes motivation and effort to distinguish the prideful promoting precepts from the pattern of humility doctrines. Many feel no need to distinguish the good from the evil.

From 2 Nephi we receive this very clear warning:

Therefore, wo be unto him that is at-ease in Zion!

Wo be unto him that crieth: All is well!

Yea, wo be unto him that hearkeneth unto the precepts of men, and denieth the power of God, and the gift of the Holy Ghost!

Yea, wo be unto him that saith: We have received, and we need no more!

» *2 Nephi 28:24-27*

We are much like the people in the parable of the nobleman and the vineyard *(D&C 101: 43-51)*. The servants were told to build a tower from which to watch the land round about, that the enemy might be seen when he was afar off, that the hedges might not be over-run and the vineyard be destroyed. But the servants decided that there was no need for the tower, and fell asleep. The hedges were overrun by the enemy and the vineyard was destroyed. Watching for the enemy and his methods today is just out of vogue. Some might even accuse us as being asleep. False doctrines, false educational ideas and Satan's adopted philosophies of men are of no concern to most. Feeling that "all is well in Zion" dominates while warnings from past prophets are ignored. Many feel "at ease" in Zion and that if any real danger does arise, a letter will be read in Sacrament Meeting.

Complacency can lead us to lose all of that which is of real worth. Alma asked some searching questions we might occasionally ask ourselves.

And now behold, I ask of you, my brethren of the church, have ye spiritually been born of God? Have ye received his image in your countenances? Have ye experienced this mighty change in your hearts?
  » *Alma 5:14*

Our Savior taught us:

Blessed are they which do hunger and thirst after righteousness: for they shall be filled.
  » *Matthew 5:6*

"Filled" with the Holy Ghost, as taught in 3 Nephi.

With a heart that has mightily changed and a hunger and thirst for righteousness, we are less likely to suffer complacency.

Worshiping the Learning of Man

During his conference address in April, 1969, Ezra Taft Benson explained.

"The world worships the learning of man. They trust in the arm of flesh. To them, men's reasoning is greater than God's revelations. The precepts of man have gone so far in subverting our educational system..."

Paul described our day and the learning of men:

Ever learning and never able to come to the knowledge of the truth.

　　» *2 Timothy 3:7*

In 2 Nephi chapter 9 verses 28-29 we read:

O that cunning plan of the evil one! O the vainness, and the frailties, and the foolishness of men! When they are learned they think they are wise, and they hearken not unto the counsel of God, for they set it aside, supposing they know of themselves, where, their wisdom is foolishness and it profiteth them not. And they shall perish.

But to be learned is good if they hearken unto the counsels of God.

The philosophers of men have not found it prudent to hearken to God's Pattern of humility, thinking that their wisdom is greater. But since they are vain and frail and foolish and hearken unto their self-focused prideful philosophies, and have such great influence, many suffer the great loss which pride always brings. This tragedy is perpetuated when good people are at ease, complacent and do not compare all things to the pattern of our Lord and continue to perpetuate prideful philosophies.

CHAPTER 9
PATTERNS OF DECEPTION

May it be perfectly clear, we need not dwell on Satan, and certainly should not dwell on evil spirits, but searching out, studying and exposing his pattern of deception is only good self-defense. The detrimental philosophies he uses should be as familiar to us as the names of our own children. When we debate, we should know the arguments of our opponent as well as we know our own. When in battle, not knowing the strategies of our foe is a formula for defeat. As we suffer the loss of great numbers of our temple marriages and our youth fail to qualify to serve their two years, we are being defeated. Not recognizing how pride is introduced into our otherwise good society allows it to spread and grow. Selfishness, a form of pride, does its great damage as humility becomes a topic often mentioned, but seldom understood, taught or discussed in-depth.

Just as there is a pattern to our Lord and Savior's teachings, certain of Satan's deceptions also follow a pattern. Some of his nefarious works are blatant and overt, such as the temptations of immorality, mind altering substances, power and greed. But for those who are trying to follow Christ, Satan knows that he must use deceptions which are much more subtle, obscure and difficult to identify. After all, he is *more subtle than any beast of the field (Genesis 3:1)*. He takes advantage of man's high esteem for the learning of men and adopts some of their philosophies to use as his own. To make them more attractive he occasionally mixes them with a little scripture. Not all philosophies of men are evil, but some are quite detrimental to men in their effort to become humble. Some are downright promoters of pride. These we can call the DPOM; the detrimental philosophies of men. His specific adopted philosophies are beyond the scope of this writing, but if we desire to know them we can each watch, compare, study and ask for help. One clue to recognizing at least one pattern of his deceptions is that they are directed toward raising the level of man's own self-perception. This is the antithesis of man's understanding his own nothingness. In such they do not align themselves with our Lord's pattern.

The real possibility of deception is something we must all consider ...*for Satan is abroad in the land...* (D&C 52:14).

...Take heed that no man deceive you.

 » *Matthew 24:4*

For there shall arise false Christs, and false prophets, and shall shew great signs and wonders; insomuch that, if it were possible, they shall deceive the very elect.

 » *Matthew 24:24*

Take heed to yourselves, that your heart be not deceived, and ye turn aside, and serve other gods, and worship them.

 » *Deuteronomy 11:16*

Wherefore, beware lest ye are deceived; and that ye may not be deceived...

 » *D&C 46:8*

And this I give unto you that you may not be deceived...

 » *D&C 43:6*

Satan is the God of all worldliness and has captured the devotion of much of the inhabitants herein. Because we must have opposition in all things, Satan is allowed to deceive us and the nations. He desires that men do not believe that he even exist. His work flourishes where people pay no attention to him or his methods. Today, many do not like to talk of him, or his methods, which only aids him in his deceptions. When his abilities and methods are ignored, by even the righteous, he is free to plant his seeds of pride and selfishness which grow, and go undetected even as they destroy blessings and tear apart families & marriages. All Satan needs to do to keep the righteous from returning to their heavenly home is introduce a little pride, and let it grow. As pride comes in, humility must exit.

> *Wherefore, he maketh war with the saints of God, and encompasseth them round about.*
> » *D&C 76:29*

Watching from a tower that the enemy might be seen before he overruns our hedges is only wise. Indeed, not knowing the particulars of what has us encompassed round about would be foolish. The war which began in heaven is still raging. Satan's DPOM permeate all corners of our society, and are widely accepted as truth. Most everyone has been deceived with at least one of these DPOM, which surround us. Each reader is encouraged to seek and identify and make their own list of the philosophies of men, of which we are so frequently warned.

Our Dictionary defines pride as: a high or inordinate opinion of one's own dignity, importance, merit, or superiority, whether as cherished in the mind or as displayed in bearing, conduct, etc. This fits the pattern of deception, that man should think highly of himself.

From Bruce R. McConkie we learn that pride "is inordinate self-esteem arising because of one's position, achievements, or possessions; and it has the effect of centering a person's heart on the things of the world rather than the things of the Spirit" *(Mormon Doctrine, first edition, p. 533).*

President Ezra Taft Benson exposed our great pride in his landmark address "Beware of Pride". General Conference April 1989 He reminds us that "Pride is the universal sin and many are sinning in ignorance". An occasional re-reading of his words can be helpful in recognizing the patterns of deception and help us monitor our own humility.

Joseph F. Smith gave us much to consider in his warning of three threatening dangers:

> "There are at least three dangers that threaten the Church within, and authorities need to awaken to the fact that the people should be warned unceasingly against them. As I see these, they are flattery of prominent men in the world , false educational ideas, and sexual impurity."
>
> » *Improvement Era, Vol. 17 No. 5. p. 476, March 1914*

Sexual impurity is a given. Flattery can encourage pride. But which are the false educational ideas he warns us about? Could they be philosophies of men which come through academia? Do we accept all that comes through the intellect of men without question, without comparing it to the pattern of our Lord? We should be able to identify those specific DPOM which foster and encourage pride and eliminate them from our teachings.

CHAPTER 10
SELF EVALUATION

This is possibly the most important chapter in this book. The topic is so important that it rates its own chapter, though it be brief. We can know all there is to know about humility, but if we do not grab the natural man by the neck and expel him from our being, we fall short of our goal. And to do that we must recognize him, as we continually watch and monitor ourselves.

✶ It is much easier to recognize pride in others, but seeing it in ourselves takes a conscious and serious effort of self-evaluation.

As a people, our pride has already been evaluated. President Ezra T. Benson has stated:

"Pride is a very misunderstood sin, and many are sinning in ignorance... It was essentially the sin of pride that kept us from establishing Zion in the days of the Prophet Joseph Smith... Pride is the stumbling block to Zion".

» *"Beware of Pride" Ensign, May 1989*

Individually, we must evaluate ourselves and "Beware of Pride". These two exact words appear three times in the Doctrine & Covenants (23:1, 25:14 and 38:39). Beyond the temptation to daily elevate ourselves above others are the far more common ailments which come from the bottom looking up, such as "faultfinding, gossiping, backbiting, murmuring, living beyond our means envying, coveting, withholding gratitude and praise that might lift another, being unforgiving and jealous" (See "Beware of Pride").

It is quite possible to possess a great deal of pride and still function quite well in religious activity. Obedience to the laws of tithing and the Word of Wisdom is often used as a gauge of worthiness, but no such examination to know of one's depth of humility exists. Nobody will likely ever ask if we have put-off pride or inquire as to our humility. If anyone is going to monitor our pride it must be us; each individual, continuing to search within him/herself for the tell-tale signs, then making the needed changes.

Here are some things to watch for:

- Are you easily offended, when corrected by your leaders or others?
- Do you have excessive concern for your own appearance?

- Do you like to show-off your possessions to others?

- Are you overly competitive?

- Do you always feel that you must be the best?

- Do you have frequent disputes with others?

- Do you not hesitate to tell others of your position, accomplishments or higher education?

- Is "self" at the top of your priority list?

- Do you enjoy talking about yourself?

- Do you love yourself?

- When others talk about themselves, do you listen with interest, or do you switch the conversation to yourself?

- Are you guilty of "faultfinding, gossiping, backbiting murmuring, living beyond your means, envying coveting, withholding gratitude and praise that might lift another, and being unforgiving and jealous"?

(See "Beware of Pride")

Or:

✓• Are you a good listener?

✓• Are you teachable?

- Do you feel humble?

✓• Do you show an interests in others, their problems and accomplishments?

- Do you seek to know what neighbor you should serve?

It is better that we start now, while times are good, to do all we can to enter into the depths of humility.

CHAPTER 11
PREPARE QUICKLY

Behold, are ye stripped of pride? I say unto you,
if ye are not ye are not prepared to meet God.
Behold ye must prepare quickly; for the kingdom
of heaven is soon at hand, and such an one hath
not eternal life.
    » *Alma 5:28*

There are two approaches to becoming humble: voluntary and involuntary. Involuntary humility comes when hardships and tragedy beset individuals or entire families. When we are struggling with prolonged illness, serious disability or extended financial problems, pride is less likely to be a problem. Deep humility often besets itself without choice. Involuntary humility is the most painful way to becoming humble. Voluntary humility is the preferred option; it is much less painful and very advisable.

Therefore, blessed are they who humble themselves
without being compelled to be humble...
  » *Alma 32:16*

Blessed is the person who chooses to become humble, all on his own because of his hunger and thirst for righteousness.

Success in almost any area can easily foster pride, making humility difficult or near impossible. Excelling in competitions and occupations can easily raise the level of a person's self-perception. Trophies indicate that you are better than everyone else. Financial success usually brings a host of worldly possessions, of which to be proud. Position, notoriety and accomplishment are often extolled by others, making humility-in-depth more difficult.

For I say... to every man that is among you, not
to think of himself more highly than he ought to
think...
  » *Romans 12:3*

One Bishop, in an affluent area of town, said that his members suffered from "afluenza". This has been an era of general prosperity, good times and without significant persecution, the perfect incubator of mass pride. Humility is the cure, and should be sought after. Much can be voluntarily done. Having faith in and following Christ's example are fundamental. We can follow the Pattern of our Lord. Throwing off pride may be the most difficult thing we ever do, that is why a "desire" for in-depth humility is needed first.

- Desire it!
- Emulate Christ! Learn His pattern!
- Put away Pride!
- Serve your neighbor! Love is not enough!
- Accept your own nothingness! Rely on the Lord!
- Abase yourself! re-read chapter 4
- Avoid groups, individuals or activities which inhibit the Spirit.
- Think of others as being better than yourself!
- Scour the scriptures! Reading and studying are good, scouring adds more!
- Fast often!
- Avoid deception by watching-out for, and avoiding:
    1. DPOM (detrimental philosophies of men) which encourage pride in self,
    2. False doctrines and
    3. False educational ideas! (One of three threats to the Church within. JFS)
- Attend the temple frequently! And listen intently!

Frequent visits to the temple, where possible, can help in different ways. One visit per month has been called "the minimum". Two visits per month is not often enough to call "frequent". But one visit per week can be powerful and:

- Help us draw closer to the Spirit,
- Help us in our Church callings,
- Help us to properly adjust our priorities,
- Help solidify our marriage relationship,
- Help us learn vital doctrines,
- Help us identify false doctrines,
- Can teach us many important precepts,
- Help us to know the kind of person we should be, and actually change who we are.

Men sometimes arrange a temple visit around their work obligations. Women sometimes go during the day, in groups. Husbands and wives can re-live the experience of their temple sealing. Visits may take as little as an hour. Giving up participation in recreational or entertainment activities can make the time available for frequent visits. Participating in all options of proxy ordinance work can be most beneficial. Family History work is an important part of temple work, but does not replace temple ordinance participation.

Come to the House of The Lord and feast on what is given. Endeavor to learn and remember all you can and time will fly. Especially while in that sacred environment, consider what positive changes you can make in your life. Give up the notion that you are wonderful and great in and of yourself (pride). Consider your own nothingness and your need to rely on your Heavenly Father and Jesus

Christ. Picture in your mind that glorious day when you return to your Heavenly Home. This is the day to prepare for that return.

CHAPTER 12
IN HIS GOOD TIME

*And if men come unto me I will show unto them
their weakness. I give unto men weakness that
they may be humble; and my grace is sufficient for
all men that humble themselves before me; for if
they humble themselves before me, and have faith
in me, then will I make weak things become strong
unto them.*

» *Ether 12:27*

*And inasmuch as they were humble they might be
made strong, and blessed from on high, and receive
knowledge from time to time.*

» *D&C 1:28*

We have these great promises, and they will for as-
suredly be fulfilled, but in His good time, not ours. In
the meantime, we must endure this life, with all of its dis-

couragements, heartaches and tragedies. We have faith to support us, but with the knowledge of what will at sometime come, if we are faithful, and humble ourselves. So in the meantime we must put–off pride, accept our own nothingness and be buoyed up by our faith and understanding of what will come. Some even now enjoy the strength humility brings, but for others, though humble, their reward may not be felt in this estate.

We can be as the young man who was asked by his mother to clean his cluttered room. He was asked repeatedly to no avail. But when he wanted to use the family car for the evening an agreement was made and he quickly obeyed. How much better it would have been if he had cleaned lie room because it was the right thing to do and because he was asked to do so, and not because he was further motivated by use of the car? How much better it is if we do things because we are commanded and not because we expect immediate rewards. That is part of the test of this life. Faith and hope should sustain us. Obedience is primary and rewards will come in His good time. Understanding our own nothingness is a great basis from which to start; everything from there is up. We can then find happiness in many small things, even from the success, happiness and blessings of others. Ammon, who understood his nothingness, enjoyed even incomprehensible joy *(Alma 28:8)*. As we follow our Lord's pattern and his example of selflessness we will learn to forget ourselves and make others our priority. In so doing, we will make our own happiness based on the sound principles of forgiveness, selflessness, service and charity. Note that each of these principles involves others. Depression can fly away and marriage relationships can become sweet, like honeycomb. As for becoming strong because we are humble, that will come in His good time.

Blessings for being obedient and humble are not limited to just becoming strong.

If ye then, being evil, know how to give good gifts unto your children, how much more shall your Father which is in heaven give good things to them that ask him?
    » *Matthew 7:11*

The scope of our potential blessings may stagger our understanding.

But as it is written, Eye hath not seen, nor ear heard, neither have entered into the heart of man, the things which God had prepared for them that love him.
    » *1 Corinthians 2:9*

...Ye shall come forth in the first resurrection...and shall inherit thrones, kingdoms, principalities, and powers, dominions, all heights and depths...
    » *D&C 132:19*

All of these may come, in His good time.

But there is one kind of blessing of which we have more immediate control. With qualification we may enjoy gifts of the spirit, on a more daily basis. These gifts range widely in their variety and are available to us all. *(See D&C 46:13-26 and 1 Corinthians 12:1-11)*. After qualifying, and having faith, the next step is to ask for them.

> *Wherefore, beware lest ye are deceived; and that ye may not be deceived seek ye earnestly the best gifts, always remembering for what they are given...*
>
> » *D&C 46:8*

We can ask for the gift of discernment, that we may recognize the philosophies and traps put in place by the Evil One. We may receive an understanding of the various philosophies of men, adopted by Satan, for our deception and destruction.

When we obey the first and great commandment *(Matthew 22:37)*, and love our Lord with all our heart, soul and mind, we will desire to obey, follow and serve Him. As we do it unto *one of the least of these (Matthew 25:40)*, we show Him our love by our service unto them. Love alone is not enough. As we adopt His pattern, we will be more inclined to forget ourselves and focus, as He did, on others. May each reader here, desire to enter into the depths of humility and hunger and thirst after righteousness, and find happiness and joy in this life and hereafter.

CHAPTER 13
FINAL THOUGHTS

One of my favorite stories from church history is an encounter between the Prophet Joseph Smith and Brigham Young. It has been handed down from Truman G. Madsen and Hugh B. Brown.

"In the presence of a rather large group of brethren, the Prophet severely chastised Brother Brigham for some failing in his duty. Everyone, I suppose somewhat stunned, waited to see what Brigham's response would be. After all, Brigham, who later became known as the Lion of the Lord, was no shrinking violet by any means. Brigham slowly rose to his feet, and in words that truly reflected his character and his humility, he simply bowed his head and said, 'Joseph, what do you want me to do?' The story goes that sobbing, Joseph ran from the podium, threw his arms around Brigham, and said in effect, 'You passed, Brother Brigham, you passed'".

» *Richard C. Edgley, "The Empowerment of Humility" Liahona November 2003 97-99*

What a great example. How many of us would have Brother Brigham's depth of humility without earnestly seek for it?

As explained above, our Lord has given us a pattern to follow: the true doctrines and teachings in the plan of happiness in His Restored Gospel. But if we are too much at ease or even asleep, and do not make the effort to compare all things, we will fail to recognize the detrimental philosophies of men (DPOM) which Satan so subtly surrounds us with, and we will be deceived. We must not consider ourselves above deception. We have been given the Holy Ghost as a comforter and a guide. Additionally, we can ask for and receive special spiritual gifts. The gift of discernment can help us see, as black from white, *the cunning and the snares and the wiles of the devil (Heleman 3:29)*. The qualifications to receive such gifts are to have sufficient faith, follow through by requesting, be worthy to have the Holy Ghost attend us and have ears to hear and eyes to see.

It is wonderful to see how all the pieces of our Lord's plan, pattern, words of His prophets, scriptures and temple teachings, fit together in such perfect harmony. May we be alert and vigilant. May we stay focused on preparing for our return to our heavenly home. May we all fill the measure of our creation by using our time on Earth wisely. May we accept our nothingness and rely on the Lord. May we each enjoy the gifts of the Spirit to help us avoid the many prideful traps. May our efforts to throw off our natural pride be successful, that we may come down, and stay, in the *depths of humility*.

Larry A. Tyler

Made in the USA
Charleston, SC
11 February 2012